Prehistoric Beasts **UNCOVERED**

Triceratops

The Dinosaur Built to Do Battle

By Dougal Dixon

RUBY TUESDAY BOOKS

Published in 2018 by Ruby Tuesday Books Ltd.

Editors: Ruth Owen and Mark Sachner
Designer: Emma Randall
Production: John Lingham

Photo Credits:
2009 Farke et al: 28 (bottom); Alamy: 8, 10 (bottom), 11 (centre), 14—15, 19 (centre), 21 (top); Black Hills Institute of Geological Research (T. Larson 2007): 13 (bottom), 19 (bottom); Tom Connell: 24—25; Eofauna: 12, 13 (top); FLPA: 23 (top); Getty Images: 29 (top); James Kuether: Cover, 4—5, 6—7, 10 (top), 11 (top), 11 (bottom), 16, 17 (top), 18, 20 (top), 22—23, 26, 31; Mississippi Department of Wildlife, Fisheries, and Parks' Museum of Natural Science: 27 (top left), 27 (bottom); Public Domain: 8 (bottom centre); 8 (bottom right), 9 (top), 19 (top), 20 (bottom), 21 (bottom right), 26; Ruby Tuesday Books: 17 (bottom), 29 (bottom); Shutterstock: 2—3, 9 (bottom), 15 (top), 15 (bottom), 17 (centre), 18, 21 (bottom left), 27 (top right), 28 (top), 29 (centre).

British Library Cataloguing In Publication Data (CIP) is available for this title.

ISBN: 978-1-911341-78-9

Printed in Poland by L&C Printing Group

www.rubytuesdaybooks.com

Contents

Naming Dinosaurs

All living things have a **Latin** scientific name in two parts – a **genus** name and a **species** name. You are *Homo sapiens*. A dog is *Canis familiaris*. It is the same with dinosaurs – for example, *Stegosaurus stenops* and *Tyrannosaurus rex*. When we speak, read or write about *Triceratops* we usually just use its genus name, but there are actually two separate species: *Triceratops horridus* (*T. horridus*) and *Triceratops prorsus* (*T. prorsus*).

Rip. Crunch. Rip. Crunch!

A small family group of *Triceratops* is grazing.
They are feeding on the ferns and flowers that
cover the plains of western North America.
It is the end of the Age of Dinosaurs,
66 million years ago.

The group is made up of five females,
several youngsters and a big male — the
leader of the herd.

Suddenly, the male stops eating.
Another huge animal appears from
out of the shade beneath some trees.

The leader of the herd stands firm.

He is ready to go
into battle. . . .

Built to do Battle

Another male *Triceratops*, a young challenger, approaches the herd leader. The challenger lowers his head and shakes his great frill so its colours stand out. The leader responds by lowering his head and showing off his own frill.

Locking Horns

The two great beasts move together. Their horns lock into one another. They shove and turn, each trying to push his opponent away from the herd. Whoever wins this battle will take the lead of the small herd, and claim mating rights with the females. With a final enormous push, the contest is won. The challenger backs off, defeated.

Theories and Evidence

Is this what took place 66 million years ago? Some of this we know. **Palaeontologists** have deduced it from **fossils** and other **evidence**. But other parts of the story are just a **theory**, good guesses based on the lives of other animals. In this book, we will uncover what we know about this huge plant-eater, and how we know it.

Discovering Triceratops

Imagine a time when rival scientists were so anxious to discover new dinosaurs that they actually fought one another to get the fame. This is exactly what happened in the late 1800s.

The Great Bone Rush

In western North America, settlers and engineers who were building railways began to find fossil bones on their land. Scientists and fossil hunters raced to these areas to dig for bones in rocky **quarries**.

Inside an animal's horn is a core of bone. A bone core was one of the first *Triceratops* fossils to be found.

Othniel Charles Marsh (back centre) with a fossil-hunting crew.

Edward Drinker Cope

The Bone Wars

Two American scientists, Othniel Charles Marsh and Edward Drinker Cope, became rivals. Their fossil-hunting crews spied on each other and stole the other crew's finds. They used dynamite to destroy each other's quarries and fossils. It was during this period, called the "bone wars", that *Triceratops* was discovered.

The First Fossils

In 1872, Cope found the hip and rib bones of a *Triceratops* in Wyoming, USA. He thought the fossils belonged to some kind of duckbilled hadrosaur. He named it *Agathaumas sylvestris*.

In 1887, Marsh was sent a pair of fossil horn cores that had been found in Colorado, USA. He decided they came from a new kind of giant prehistoric buffalo, which he named *Bison alticornis*. They were both wrong!

A sketch of the fossil horn cores and skull that were studied by Marsh

Rough Three-horned Head

In 1888, a more complete skull was discovered. Marsh realised that all the fossils came from the same kind of animal. He named it *Triceratops horridus*, which means "rough three-horned head".

Many Different Triceratops?

In the decades that followed Marsh's naming of *Triceratops*, more skulls were found. Many were slightly different from one another. Scientists believed they were different kinds of *Triceratops*, and about fifteen different species were named. It was only in the 1980s that scientists understood that a *Triceratops*'s skull could change shape as it grew up. Today we think there are only two true species – *Triceratops horridus* and *Triceratops prorsus*.

An American bison

Meet the Family

Triceratops was the biggest member of the group of horned dinosaurs called the ceratopsians. The earliest ceratopsians lived in Asia and did not look much like *Triceratops*. Their fossils have been found in rocks that formed during the **Jurassic period**.

Hidden Dragon

Yinlong means "hidden dragon" in Chinese. Long is Chinese for "dragon" and often forms part of the name of a Chinese dinosaur.

Yinlong

Yinlong was a fox-sized animal with a deep, wide skull and long legs for running. A special bone at the tip of its upper jaw shows that it was a ceratopsian, even though it had no frill or horns.

When: 160 million years ago
Where: China

Sinraptor

Yinlong

Psittacosaurus

Psittacosaurus was the size of a labrador and had a big, parrot-like beak. Its name means "parrot lizard". Some **specimens** are so well preserved they have a great array of porcupine-like quills along the tail.

When: 126 million years ago
Where: Mongolia and China

The Horned Giants

By the end of the **Cretaceous period** the ceratopsians had spread from Asia into North America. Most of them had become much bigger. They all had the same body shape, but with different arrangements of horns and frill.

Styracosaurus means "spiked lizard".

Styracosaurus

Styracosaurus had a single huge horn on its nose, no brow horns and a splendid array of six spikes around the edge of its frill.

Kosmoceratops

Kosmoceratops had a square frill with a row of forward-curving spikes on the top edge.

Kosmoceratops's name means "ornamented horn-head".

The Last Ceratopsian

The last of the ceratopsians was *Triceratops*. It lived in North America right up to the end of the Age of Dinosaurs, 66 million years ago.

Leptoceratops

There were still some small ceratopsians around in the late Cretaceous period. *Leptoceratops* was the size of a sheep and had no horns or frill.

Meet Triceratops

With a massive elephant-sized body, *Triceratops* was the biggest of the ceratopsians.

Four Strong Legs

Triceratops's front legs were shorter than its back legs. This suggests it **evolved** from two-footed **ancestors** that only walked on their strong back legs. Its elbows were bent. Scientists know this from studying *Triceratops* trackways preserved in rock. The tracks show that its front feet were slightly further apart than the back feet.

The front feet had five toes. The animal's weight was carried on three of the toes, which were equipped with weight-bearing hooves.

How Big?

Triceratops was about 9 metres long. Scientists can only estimate its weight, but it's possible an adult weighed up to 12,000 kilograms — the same weight as 12 rhinos!

Each back foot had four hoofed toes.

The back legs were held directly under the animal and carried most of its weight.

From the curve of *Triceratops*'s ribs, we can see that its ribcage was very wide and barrel-shaped. This tells us that just like a modern-day cow, *Triceratops* had a very large **digestive system**. It probably had more than one stomach and many metres of **intestines**. This was needed because digesting plant material is a longer and more complicated process than digesting meat.

Muscle Scars

Scientists can work out the shape and size of *Triceratops*'s muscles by looking at "muscle scars". These are marks on the fossilised bones where muscles were attached.

Bone

Muscles

Fossilised *Triceratops* skin

The scales fitted together like the sections of a football.

Some scales have cone-like projections.

A Scaly *Triceratops*

In 2002, scientists **excavated** a *Triceratops* skeleton in Wyoming, USA. They discovered something that had never been seen before – *Triceratops* skin. Until this time, scientists imagin that *Triceratops* had either tough, smooth skin, like an elephant, or skin covered in small **scales**. The fossilised skin showed that *Triceratops*'s body was covered in large scales. Some of the largest measure 10 centimetres

Rough, Three-Horned Head

The most recognisable feature of a *Triceratops* is its enormous head. And what a head it was!

A Solid Skull

It's very rare to find a fossilised dinosaur skull. Most skulls were made of many light pieces of bone. After a dinosaur died, its skull fell to pieces and the bits became scattered before it could fossilise. This was not the case with *Triceratops*. Its skull was so solid it's more likely to be found than the rest of the skeleton. To date, more than 50 *Triceratops* skulls have been found.

Two long, forward-pointing brow horns

Short nose horn

Nostril opening

Narrow, hard, parrot-like beak

Skull could reach a length of 2.5 metres from the beak to the edge of the frill.

Teeth

Cheek area

Big Nose

The space in a *Triceratops*'s skull that held the nostril was huge. The open space was covered by skin, with a small nostril hole quite far forward. Bony structures inside the cavity may have supported moist tissue that cooled the air as it was breathed in. They may even have supported balloon-like structures used for making noises like a frog. No one can say for sure.

Could a *Triceratops* inflate its nostril skin as a frog does with its throat skin?

Huge bony frill

A Patterned Frill

Triceratops's neck frill was so big scientists agree it must have been used to display to other members of its kind. This means it was probably brightly coloured and patterned.

A Tough Covering

Triceratops's upper skull, horns and bony frill were covered in tough **keratin**. We know this because of the surface texture of the bone. Keratin is the same material that forms an antelope's horns, a bird's beak and your fingernails. The outer layer of keratin would have flaked off constantly and been replaced by new layers that grew from the bone.

Cheek Pouches?

A *Triceratops*'s teeth are not on the edge of the mouth but inset a little. Scientists think that the animal's cheeks covered its teeth. This created a pouch-like space where food could be held as it was chewed.

Beak made of keratin

15

Horns for Battle

Triceratops's horns were formidable weapons. They were long, strong and pointed — but what were they used for?

Horns for Defence

The giant plant-eater's horns could have been used for fending off the biggest meat-eating dinosaur around at the time — the fearsome *Tyrannosaurus rex*. However, scientists have never found any evidence that the two great beasts fought.

Dead or Alive?

Scientists have found toothmarks on *Triceratops* bones that match *T. rex*'s teeth. This proves *Triceratops* was eaten by *T. rex*. But it doesn't tell us if *T. rex* hunted and attacked *Triceratops*. It could be that *T. rex* feasted from the carcass of a *Triceratops* that had already died.

A *T. rex* pursuing a young *Triceratops*. Fact or fiction? For now, we don't know!

Who's the Boss?

Big male *Triceratops* may have used their horns in battles to win leadership of a herd. These fights would not have been to the death, just to establish which animal was the strongest.

Some *Triceratops* skulls have holes that match the horn tips of other *Triceratops*. It's possible to see that the injuries healed and new bone grew. This means that the loser of the fight did not die.

This hole was made by a *Triceratops*'s horn!

The horns of some sheep grow curly as they get longer.

Bigger Than They Look

In life, *Triceratops*'s bony horn cores were covered in tough keratin. As new keratin formed at the base of the horns, they grew longer and longer. In fact, *Triceratops*'s horns were possibly twice the length of the cores. This is exactly how the horns of buffalo and antelopes are formed.

Keratin Horn

Bone core

A *Triceratops* With Curls?

As *Triceratops*'s horns grew longer, they may even have become curly. But that is only a theory. The keratin part of the horns rotted after death, leaving only the bony cores behind to become fossils.

A *Triceratop*'s brow horns could grow to 1 metre long.

17

Triceratops Food

Triceratops was a plant-eater that lived on open **prairies**. With its head held close to the ground, it ate low-growing vegetation such as ferns and the first small flowering plants. It also fed on low-growing palms and cycads.

Slicing and Chopping

Triceratops teeth worked in a scissor action. They slid past each other and chopped mouthfuls of plant material into little pieces. The pieces were probably held in the animal's cheek pouches and chopped again and again until the food was ready to swallow.

Cycad

Picking Out the Best Bits

Triceratops's narrow beak must have been used for selecting choice pieces of plant to eat, such as the growing hearts of cycads.

Tender new leaves in the growing heart of a cycad

Tough Teeth

If we cut open a fossilised *Triceratops* tooth we find that it was made of five layers of bony material. Reptiles have only two layers and humans have three. The modern plant-eaters with the strongest teeth, such as horses and buffalo, have a maximum of four layers. This shows us that *Triceratops* was able to slice through some very tough plants. This allowed it to eat foods not available to other plant-eaters.

Lower jaw of
Triceratops

This area of the tooth has been worn flat by slicing through tough plants.

Triceratops tooth

Hundreds of Teeth

The chopping action put a lot of strain on *Triceratops*'s teeth and they wore out quickly. When a tooth dropped out, it was immediately replaced by a fresh tooth growing out of a stack within the jawbone. With all these teeth growing continuously, an adult *Triceratops* had between 400 and 800 teeth in its jaws at a time.

These teeth were in use when the animal died.

Replacement teeth stacked in the jawbone

Triceratops Grows Up

More than 50 *Triceratops* skulls have been discovered in the past 130 years. They come in a wide range of sizes and shapes.

A baby *Triceratops*

Growing and Changing

Today, we know what a baby *Triceratops* looked like. The fossilised skulls have also shown us that a *Triceratops*'s skull, frill and horns changed as it grew up.

Tiny, stumpy horns

Hardly any frill

A Baby Triceratops

The smallest *Triceratops* baby that's been found had a skull that was 38 centimetres long. It's possible that its body was covered in spiky feathers. Its tail may have had quills like some of its early relatives. This is just a guess, however. There is no evidence.

A Growing *Triceratops*

As a *Triceratops* became a juvenile, the bones around the back of its skull spread outwards and began to form its frill. Knobbly, **ornamental** sections formed on the edge of the frill. Its three horns started to grow, but at this stage, its brow horns curved backwards.

Ornamental sections on the frill

Backwards-facing horns

Becoming an Adult

As a *Triceratops* grew, its brow horns became longer and the frill became broader. As it approached adulthood, a *Triceratops*'s horns began to grow forwards. The frill changed, too, and no longer had ornamental knobbly sections.

A juvenile *Triceratops*

A *Torosaurus* skull

A *Torosaurus*

To Be Continued. . . .

It's possible there was another growth stage in the life of *Triceratops*. A big ceratopsian named *Torosaurus* lived alongside *Triceratops* at the same time. It had a much longer bony frill with two holes in it. But was *Torosaurus* actually a *Triceratops* that had reached old age? Did *Triceratops*'s frill continue to grow and then form holes to reduce its weight? It's an important theory, but not all scientists agree.

Family Life

Triceratops is the most common dinosaur fossil found in North American rocks, but we actually know very little about how it lived. For now, scientists can only make guesses about its life based on the lives of its relatives and other animals.

How the Relatives Lived

In Texas, fossils of a *Chasmosaurus* herd were found. *Chasmosaurus* was an early relative of *Triceratops*. Scientists think the herd died together in a sudden disaster, such as a flood. They discovered the herd consisted of one adult, some sub-adults, some medium-sized animals and several youngsters. However, there were no bones from newborns or very young animals.

An Adult Triceratops

Examining Clues

The scientists who studied the fossils of the *Chasmosaurus* herd measured the lengths of the femurs (thigh bones) that were found amongst the scattered fossils. From this, they were able to estimate the sizes of the animals.

These pictures show the growth stages of *Triceratops*. The animals' sizes have been calculated based on fossil finds.

Baby

Juvenile

22

A herd of musk oxen ready to defend against a predator.

All for One, And One for All

Did a group of *Triceratops* work as a team, using their horns, to defend each other and their young? It's an interesting idea that's based on the behaviour of modern-day musk oxen. When under attack from a predator, these powerful animals form a tightly packed circle with their huge horned heads facing outwards. The herd's calves huddle together inside the circle of giant adults. Perhaps a *Triceratops* family protected its young in the same way.

Sub-adult

More Clues Needed

What do the bones of the *Chasmosaurus* herd tell us? Perhaps it shows that baby *Chasmosaurus* lived away from the herd with their mothers. Once the babies had grown a little, the mothers and babies rejoined the main herd.

Did *Triceratops* have this kind of herd structure? More evidence is needed.

Finding Bones

Sometimes palaeontologists discover a mixed-up jumble of bones from several animals. This is called a bone bed.

A bone bed probably formed when a whole herd of animals died at the same time in a catastrophic event. Maybe the animals

1) As a migrating herd of *Centrosaurus* crosses a river, a flash flood washes away many of the animals.

2) The bodies are carried downstream.

Death By Drowning

If a ceratopsian was caught in a flood, it probably drowned because of its frill and horns. It would not have been able to lift its heavy head above the water to breathe.

A group of *Styracosaurus* defend their young against predators.

The floods leave behind layers of sand and mud. If you cut a slice through the land, it's possible to see the layers that have built up over thousands of years.

Deeper underground are the remains of animals killed in a flood thousands of years ago. Their bones have become fossils, buried in a bone bed. The bones are laid down orientated in the direction of the river current.

were caught in a flash flood as the herd crossed a river. A storm may have caused the sea to surge over a coastal plain, drowning a herd of grazing animals. The dinosaurs most often found in bone beds are ceratopsians.

We don't know yet if *Triceratops* moved about in herds, but most of the other big ceratopsians did. Huge herds of *Centrosaurus* **migrated** from inland areas to the coast, possibly to find fresh food supplies.

3) The bodies are washed up on sandbanks. Big tyrannosaurs and pterosaurs feed on the bodies. The *Centrosaurus* skeletons get trampled and broken up.

4) When the next flood comes, the bones are carried away by the river. They settle on the riverbed. In time they will become a bone bed.

The river constantly changes its course. Underground it's possible to see a layer of sand that shows where the river used to flow.

Uncovering Clues, Changing History

By finding and excavating fossils, scientists can work out where dinosaurs lived. Sometimes, however, a fossil is found that changes everything we thought we knew!

During the Cretaceous period, North America was divided by a sea into two great land masses, Laramidia and Appalachia. Fossils of ceratopsians had only ever been found in western North America. This led palaeontologists to believe that *Triceratops* and its relatives only lived in Laramidia.

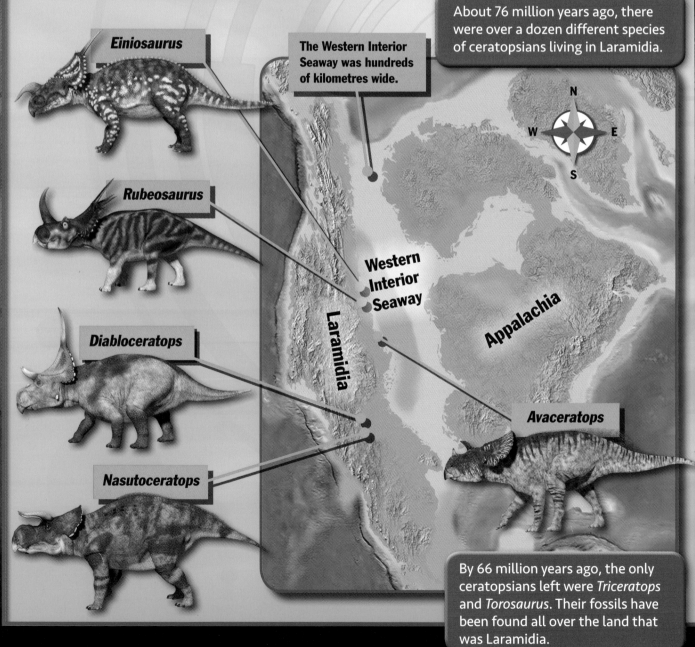

Einiosaurus

Rubeosaurus

Diabloceratops

Nasutoceratops

The Western Interior Seaway was hundreds of kilometres wide.

Western Interior Seaway

Laramidia

Appalachia

Avaceratops

About 76 million years ago, there were over a dozen different species of ceratopsians living in Laramidia.

By 66 million years ago, the only ceratopsians left were *Triceratops* and *Torosaurus*. Their fossils have been found all over the land that was Laramidia.

Uncovering a Mystery

In 2017, palaeontologist George Phillips found a fossilised tooth in a stream in Mississippi, USA. It was soon identified as belonging to a ceratopsian — maybe even *Triceratops*! The mystery was how did a ceratopsian tooth end up in eastern North America?

North America today

The tooth was found in Mississippi.

The ceratopsian tooth

A New Home

There can only be one answer — ceratopsians also lived in Appalachia. One theory is that at the very end of the Cretaceous period, the sea that separated Laramidia from Appalachia was receding, or draining away. This allowed dinosaurs in the west to spread to the east.

Tiny Tooth, Huge Discovery

A tooth is a tiny discovery, but for dinosaur science it's huge. It tells scientists that ceratopsians may have lived all over North America. This could mean there are more fossils to be discovered in places where scientists have never looked before.

One day this small find could lead to more discoveries that completely change the story of *Triceratops*!

The tooth discovered in Mississippi

A *Triceratops* lower jaw

Testing *Triceratops*

Once a *Triceratops* fossil is in a **laboratory**, all kinds of scientific techniques can be used to learn more about the animal.

Horns for Fighting

We now know that *Triceratops* used their horns to fight with each other. But how did scientists prove this was the case?

Playing with Dinosaurs

In 2009, a research team used a pair of plastic model dinosaurs to recreate battles between *Triceratops*. The scientists bashed the model dinosaurs into each other to see what damage would be done.

The team carefully noted where a *Triceratops*'s horns impacted with its opponent's head and frill. Next, the scientists looked for damage in those same places on real fossil skulls. The research team found damage caused by horns in the places they had predicted.

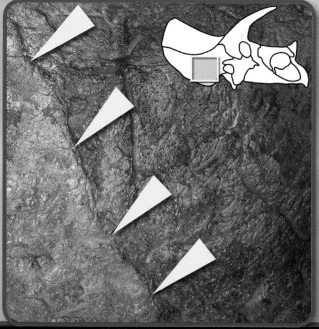

The yellow arrow shows a horn impact below a *Triceratops*'s eye.

These arrows show damage caused to a *Triceratops*'s frill.

Tough Teeth

An animal that eats tough plants, like grass, must have strong teeth. A horse's teeth are made up of layers of different materials. The layers wear away at different rates. This creates a very rough, bumpy chewing surface that acts like a vegetable grater. Scientists wanted to know if a *Triceratops*'s teeth wore out in the same way.

Grass is very tough to chew because it contains microscopic particles of a rocky material called silica.

Triceratops Goes to the Dentist

To recreate a *Triceratops* feeding, the research team used a drill-like tool with a super-hard tip made of diamond. They ran the tool across the chewing surface of a *Triceratops* tooth again and again. The experiment showed that the tooth was made up of layers of five different materials. Each layer was a different hardness. Just like a horse's tooth, the different layers wore away at different rates, developing a vegetable grater-like surface. This proved that *Triceratops*'s teeth were designed to eat plant material that was very, very tough.

A microtribometer

Diamond-tipped tool

Triceratops tooth

Glossary

ancestor
An animal that is related to one that exists in a later period of time.

Cretaceous period
A period in time that came between the Jurassic period and the Paleogene period. It lasted from 145.5 million years ago to 66 million years ago. The Cretaceous period was the end of the Age of Dinosaurs.

digestive system
The stomach, intestines and other organs that digest food.

evidence
Information that can be used to show that something is true. For example, differently shaped fossil skulls are evidence that *Triceratops*'s head changed shape as it grew.

evolve
To change or develop slowly, often over a long period of time.

excavate
To dig into the ground to uncover something, such as a fossil.

fossil
The hard remains of a living thing that are preserved in rock.

genus
A classification of living things. A genus may cover several species. For example, the genus *Panthera* includes *Panthera leo*, the lion, and *Panthera tigris*, the tiger.

intestines
The long tube that forms part of the digestive system. Water and nutrients from food are absorbed into the body from the intestines.

Jurassic period
The second of the three periods of the Mesozoic era, from 200 to 145 million years ago. This was the heyday of the Age of Dinosaurs.

keratin
A tough, natural material that is found in hair and nails, and forms animal body parts such as hooves and beaks.

laboratory
A room or building where there is equipment that can be used to carry out experiments and other scientific studies.

Latin
A language that began in ancient Rome. Scientists still use Latin today when naming animals, plants and other living things.

migrate
To move from one place to another and then back again in order to find food and mates, or to avoid extreme weather conditions.

ornamental
For decoration only.

palaeontologist
A scientist who studies animals and plants from the past.

prairie
A large area of flat land with low-growing plants and few trees.

quarry
A large hole that has been excavated in the ground, or a place where a cliff or mountain slope has been dug out to obtain rock or to find fossils.

scales
Thin, tough, flat plates, or sections, of skin that form the covering of an animal.

species
Different types of living things. The members of an animal species look alike and can produce young together.

specimen
A sample of something used for scientific study.

theory
An idea or belief that is based on limited information. A theory can be proved with evidence.

Index

Learn More Online
Could you be a scientist uncovering the buried secrets of prehistoric beasts?
Go to: www.rubytuesdaybooks.com/dinosaurs